Conflict & Concord

Bishop Humphrey Southern
Sister Susan SLG
Sister Rosemary SLG
Professor Bronwen Neil
Sister Clare-Louise SLG

First edition 2014

Fairacres Publications 219

ISBN 978-0-7283-0389-8
Fairacres Publications Series ISSN 0307-1405

Edited and typeset in Palatino Linotype by Julia Craig-McFeely

SLG Press
Convent of the Incarnation
Fairacres • Oxford
www.slgpress.co.uk

Printed by
Grosvenor Group Ltd, Loughton, Essex

CONTENTS

Preface

How do we understand, how do we deal with, the unpleasantness, the injustice, cruelty and just plain evil that we see around us every day? How do we govern the passions that lead to these things and that we feel in response: grief, fear, desperation and even anger?

The articles of the Summer 2023 issue of the *Fairacres Chronicle* came together to address these problems; to look at the reasons for human actions, the way our passions and frailties make us feel and behave, and what Christian faith offers as help, particularly as part of a life of prayer and reconciliation. This group of articles written and drawing on sources that spread over many years spoke with particular immediacy to world events at the time of the Chronicle and, sadly, to world events at almost any time in the last century and more. An understanding of anger and hatred and what it can do to us, but also how we can manage and redirect those feelings, how we can bring these things to God, never lacks currency. Publishing these articles as a book is a response both to the difficulties of our world and to our personal anguish about them, reminding us to seek answers, solace and reason in the arms of the Comforter.

ACKNOWLEDGEMENTS

The Extinguishment of the Ordinary: sermon preached at the Convent of the Incarnation, Fairacres, Oxford, on Sunday 29 October 2023, the last Sunday after Trinity.

Augustine on the Lord's Prayer: paper given at the SLG Companions Day, October 2023.

The Holy Cross: sermon preached at the Convent of the Incarnation, Fairacres, Oxford, for the feast of the Holy Cross 2024.

How to Live with the Passions: revised and updated version of an article originally published online but no longer available, 'The Blessed Passion of Holy Love: The Spiritual Psychology of Maximus the Confessor', *Australian eJournal of Theology,* 2 (February 2004).

SSJE, SLG and the Heart: drawn from the addresses given at the 2023 SLG Llangasty Retreat.

Conflict & Concord

The Extinguishment of the Ordinary

Bishop Humphrey Southern

'The last Sunday of ordinary time' is a phrase with a somewhat apocalyptic ring to it, perhaps, especially in such extraordinary times as these. The last Sunday of the green season against a backdrop of black smoke, spilled red blood, grey grief etched on the faces of the traumatized and bereaved, the burnt umber hues of climate change and the muddiness of the flood waters. The end—it is all too tempting to think—of all colour, all hope and all promise: the extinguishment of the ordinary that has kept us going.

I wonder if I should be apologizing for this bleakness? Seeking to relieve it, or ignore it, or even deny it? Or perhaps it is the case that these days—Gaza and Ukraine, US gun crime and universal climate disaster and all the rest of it notwithstanding—are not so very extraordinary, after all, just days and times like any other. Though I am not sure there would be much comfort in such a conclusion.

No. I think we do need to acknowledge the parlousness of our world—whether in fact (as if misery were measurable) it is any more or less the case in these times than any other—and ask the insistent and essential theological questions: 'Where is God? What has God got to say as ordinary time comes to an end, as extraordinary challenge and grief and terror confront the world?'

Where is God? And what has God got to say? What is God's will in these circumstances, and how might we discern how to be obedient to it? What is at the heart of God's Good News? Even—especially—in such times as these. Or (to put it another way, as did the lawyer in Matthew 22:34–46) which is the greatest commandment in God's law for our times, for all times?

Jesus's answer, as we know, was orthodox, succinct and comprehensive: 'Love the Lord your God with all your heart, with all your soul and with all your mind ... and ... love your neighbour as yourself.' (Matt. 22:37–9). Orthodox, succinct, comprehensive and—it may be added—next to impossible! Simple in concept, without doubt, but devastatingly difficult, as the world and many of us, and certainly I, have found in experience.

When we recall that just a few pages back in the same Gospel Jesus made it abundantly clear that this 'neighbour' means and includes our enemy, the one who does and wishes us evil, the point becomes all the more obvious.

Palestinian, love the Israeli soldier who is dispossessing you and raining bombs down upon your hospitals and refuges. Kibbutzim, pray for and wish well the terrorist who brought mayhem and death to your peaceful community, your idyllic late summer music festival. Ukrainian, love the invader. President Putin, embrace those whom you most fear.

This—this extraordinary instruction—is the ordinary ethic for the Kingdom of God, for these and for all times. It is the ethic to inform our politics and our public judgements as much as our private relationships and personal decisions. This, too, is the standard by which we and our world (and our generation) will be judged.

'Ordinary Time' in the calendar of the Church gives way to the modern, relatively recently-minted, 'Kingdom Season'. It is a time for reflection on what God's rule entails, what God's justice calls out for. It is a season, as is Advent, which follows as the new liturgical year is ushered in, in which the uncomfortable notion of Judgement is prominent and unavoidable. The themes in Matthew's Gospel from chapter 22 on become steadily darker and more minatory, with religious and social structures condemned by Jesus: 'woe to you, scribes and Pharisees' (Matt. 23:25); Jerusalem and its temple, heart and epicentre of order and nation, foretold for destruction: 'not one stone will be left upon another' (Matt. 24:2); violent separation and upset promised: 'Two women will be grinding meal together: one will be taken and one left … keep awake, therefore…' (Matt. 24:41).

The section of Matthew's Gospel ends with that extraordinary chapter 25, at once both terrifying and mystifying, yet also so simple in its application: the parable of the silly girls who miss a party, the cowardly and risk-averse steward who fails to invest and so loses his all, and the sheep and the goats who had no idea who was among them, or whose law was judging them.

Judgement, division, loss ... and promise. Extraordinary and bleak themes, yes, for these extraordinary and bleak times through which we and our world are passing.

Where is truth? Where hope? What is the Divine saying?

My God, my God, why have you forsaken [us]?

That, surely, is the heart of the utterance. The cry of agony and despair that reveals—in the very Broken One who utters it—the very presence and promise of God, which is our only hope.

And what do we do in this presence, in the noonday darkness of our experience, as the fabric, not just of the temple curtain but of our whole security (as it may seem) is torn in two? Why, love God, that's what. And love our neighbour as ourselves. It is as simple as that!

Bishop Humphrey Southern read history at Christ Church Oxford. In 1983 He went to Ripon College Cuddesdon for three years of ordination training. He was appointed Bishop of Repton in the diocese of Derby in May 2007. He chaired the Mission and Pastoral Committee and enjoyed close involvement with schools, chairing the Diocesan Board of Education for two years. He was appointed Principal of Cuddesdon Theological College in April 2015 where he teaches Pastoral Theology.

Augustine on the Lord's Prayer

Sister Susan SLG

Sister Benedicta Ward SLG once told me that all the early Fathers wrote about the Lord's Prayer. I am not sure if that is literally true, though I do know that a number did. I think she wanted to stress how important the prayer was for the Early Church. I, in my turn, have been wanting to look further into it for some time. I have chosen St Augustine of Hippo because his writings on the Lord's Prayer are the first of those commentaries that I have looked at in any depth.

Augustine (354–430) preached or wrote about the Lord's Prayer in three places: in his commentary on the Sermon on the Mount, in his letter to Proba, and in sermons, particularly numbers 56–9. The commentary on the Sermon on the Mount was possibly his earliest biblical commentary and covers Matthew 5–7. Scholars have suggested that it was written to fill out the teaching he had given in sermons, and that seems likely. Proba, on the other hand, was a wealthy widow in exile from the Vandals who were approaching Rome. She had written to Augustine to ask how we should pray and what we should pray for. A short commentary on the Lord's Prayer is part of his answer. The sermons are, in some ways, the most interesting, as they were intended mainly for candidates for baptism and delivered at least two weeks before Easter, the day on which they would be baptized. The candidates had already been 'given' the creed and on the previous Sunday had 'given it back', that is, they proved they knew it by reciting it. Now they were learning the Lord's Prayer, and they would recite that too on the following Sunday. The unfamiliar concept of being given a prayer and then giving it back is perhaps significant: the Lord's Prayer was a gift.

This idea of a gift can be felt right at the beginning of the prayer: it is addressed to *Our Father*. This is something new: calling God 'Father' is an innovation in the New Testament; it does not happen in the Scriptures we call the Old Testament. In addition, though, there is the word 'our'. What do we mean when we use that word, when we say it in the context of the prayer? I suppose I have always thought of the people I am saying it with at that moment, and indeed Christians everywhere, much as we say 'We believe' at the beginning of the Creed and start the confession with 'We confess'. However, Augustine points out a deeper meaning: for him it is an expression of relationship to Jesus. God is father to Jesus, so if we too say *our Father*, we are Jesus's brothers and sisters. He writes, that,

> Our Lord Jesus Christ is the only Son of God, still for all that he didn't want to be the one and only; he thought it proper to have brothers and sisters. And who did he want us to call our Father, if not his own Father?[1]

So God is our Father, and we are brothers and sisters of Jesus, but God, as Father, is described as being in heaven. When we were children, 'heaven' may have made us think of a great distance above us, but as adults it may be more of a puzzle. What is Augustine thinking when he says the prayer and describes the Father as heavenly, or in heaven? Perhaps he did have an understanding of the cosmology of his time when he refers to the 'lofty bodies of the universe', but here he makes it clear that he has a more earthly concept in mind. He quotes St Paul, 'for it is said to the righteous "the temple of God is holy, which temple you are"' (1 Cor. 3:17 AV),[2] and he goes on to say,

> the expression '*Our Father Who art in heaven*', is rightly understood to mean that He is in the hearts of the just, as though in His holy temple.[3]

---

[1] Sermon 57.2, in *Sermons III (51–94)*, trans. with notes Edmund Hill OP (New City, 1991). For the sake of fluency in reading I have not always indicated breaks in the quoted texts with an ellipsis.

[2] *Sermon on the Mount* II, 5.17, in *Commentary on the Lord's Sermon on the Mount with Seventeen Related Sermons*, trans. Denis J. Kavanagh OSA, The Fathers of the Church 11 (Catholic University of America, 1951).

[3] *Sermon on the Mount* II, 5.18, trans. Kavanagh.

Augustine says this phrase also means that when we are engaged in prayer we should wish that He whom we are invoking may dwell in us also, and that we should hold fast to righteousness while we are striving for this indwelling. So, when we say 'Our Father in heaven' we are inviting God to dwell in us, and heaven in fact is, or can be, within us, as well as far beyond us.

By speaking of righteousness Augustine has introduced an element of morality, of how we should behave, into his exposition. He continues with that thought of how we should live, with:

> Hallowed be Thy Name,
> Thy kingdom come,
> Thy will be done on earth as in heaven.

In Augustine's mind these three petitions are connected. To make any real sense we have to mean, 'may your name be made holy in me', or perhaps, 'may I be made holy by the use and knowledge of your name'. In the same way we have to mean, 'may your kingdom be found in me', and lastly, 'may I do your will':

> You are requesting something good for yourself, you are praying for yourself. What you are longing for, what you are setting your heart on by this prayer, is that you may live in such a way as to belong to the kingdom of God, which is to be given to all the Saints. So you are praying for yourself, that you may live a good life, when you say, 'Thy kingdom come'. May we belong to your kingdom; may it also come to us, the kingdom that is going to come to your holy ones.[4]

This interpretation is strong and, I find, helpful; after all, one can only change, reform oneself; but all three petitions must also have universal meaning: 'may your name be held holy throughout the world and your kingdom come, everywhere'.

The last of the three, the obedience to the will of God, introduces the problem of heaven again and Augustine's solution is similar to the one he gave us for 'Our Father in heaven': he says heaven is the Church, earth the Church's enemies: 'May our enemies believe as we

[4] Sermon 56.6, trans. Hill.

too believe in you; may they become friends, and put a stop to hostilities.'[5] Could anything be more apt today?

We come next to 'Give us this day our daily bread'. We have to remember that for the people of antiquity bread was the staple food in a way that, at least here in the West today, it is not. Without bread the poor starved. Augustine, however, believes that bread does not just mean food; it is quite clear that for him it means everything that supplies the needs of life, physical and spiritual, and he seems to refer to a daily eucharist:

> the faithful also know a spiritual sustenance, which you too are going to know, and to receive from the altar of God. That too will be a daily bread necessary for this life.[6]

Jesus's use of the word 'daily', however, makes a link with another strand of His teaching, that about anxiety and trust, epitomized perhaps in 'take no thought for the morrow' (Matt. 6:34 AV), which is a saying that poses some problems for most of us. Augustine's answer is that, providing we are working for the Kingdom, we may amass food or goods but not if we are doing it for personal security or comfort.

> Therefore, anything that is sought for the sake of something else is undoubtedly inferior to the object for which it is sought. Consequently, if we are seeking the Gospel and the kingdom of God for the sake of food, we are giving food priority and then afterwards the kingdom of God; the upshot is that, if there were no lack of food, we would not seek the kingdom of God.[7]

There is the example of the prophet Agabus who foresaw a famine and St Paul authorized a collection to help the people of Judea (Acts 11:28).

[5] Sermon 56.8, trans. Hill.

[6] Sermon 57.7, trans. Hill.

[7] *Sermon on the Mount* II, 16.55, translated in 'The Lord's Sermon on the Mount', trans. Michael G. Campbell, in *The New Testament I and II*, The Works of Saint Augustine: A Translation for the 21st Century vols. 15–16, ed. Boniface Ramsey (New City, 2014), 9–130.

The fifth petition is one Augustine returns to repeatedly in various writings: 'Forgive us our sins' (or debts). The repetition is so frequent and strong that I wondered in fact if this petition, with its vital qualifying clause, 'as we forgive those who sin against us', should be the whole subject of this essay. The fact that I considered that is an indication of just how strongly Augustine conveys his thoughts on the subject in his writings.

In his commentary on the Sermon on the Mount Augustine speaks about forgiving actual monetary debt. We are, he says, to remit the debt of someone who refuses to repay it, whether it is because he does not have any money with which to repay it, or because he is avaricious and covetous. Each reason arises from a lack of something: the first from a lack of means, the second from a lack of character. Both types of debtors are people in need.[8] Whoever, therefore, forgives such a person's debt is forgiving a poor person and performing a Christian act. Augustine refers again to St Paul, quoting from 2 Tim. 2:24: 'It is not fitting … for a servant of the Lord to engage in litigation' (2 Tim 2:24).[9] When he moves on to other kinds of sin, Augustine emphasizes that forgiveness applies to all of us, even the bishop, because although all our sins are forgiven at baptism, as we go on living we contract other sins or debts which need to be forgiven every day. He uses the metaphor of pumping out the bilges: if a boatman neglects to do that the water will rise to a dangerous level in his boat.[10] Augustine is talking about the little daily sins which plague us all: he says even if we can shut our eyes, ears and tongues to little sins, there are still our thoughts. Can we control these? He concludes that as we all have these little daily sins, we all 'have to say, as a kind of daily wash and brush up, "forgive us our sins as we too forgive those who sin against us"'.[11]

I wondered whether it was Augustine's experience of the church and monastic communities that brought him so strongly to this

[8] *Sermon on the Mount* II, 8.28, trans. Kavanagh.

[9] Ibid.

[10] Sermon 56.11, trans. Hill.

[11] Sermon 56.14, trans. Hill.

realization. That is not true if I am claiming that it was community life alone; if you have read the *Confessions* you will know that Augustine came to the realization of sin as a young man—possibly as a teenager—and, like St Paul, he found that human beings are inwardly conflicted: we cannot, or do not, do what we really want (Rom. 7:25). But let us consider community, whether one like SLG, or the community of our Churches or families, or any other group to which we belong. There is the daily friction between people who irritate each other and our tendency to give it voice or turn it into action. There may also be a sense of constriction, against which we may react, because all types of community have ground rules whether explicit or implicit. On the last Sunday before Lent the Orthodox Church keeps 'Forgiveness Sunday' when the congregation has the opportunity during the liturgy to apologize to other members of the church individually. I expect it can be misused, but nevertheless it says something about forgiveness, something about the reality of forgiveness: it is not just a pious aspiration, it is an attempt to make forgiveness a reality, and to love our enemies.[12]

The final petition, 'lead us not into temptation', is followed immediately by 'but deliver us from evil', which Augustine sometimes treats as two petitions, but sometimes takes together as one. The obvious problem here is 'can a good God be said to lead us into temptation?' Augustine's answer is not that God himself tempts us, but that He allows us to be tested.[13] He quotes various texts to explain this interpretation; the one that speaks to me most deeply is from the book of Sirach in the Apocrypha, 'what sort of things does that person know who has never been tempted?' (Sir. 34:9 Vulgate), but he also quotes John 6:6, 'He said this to test him, for he himself knew what he was going to do'. Augustine continues:

> ... undoubtedly the reason for that was that he who was being tested would grow in self-knowledge and be critical of his lack of faith, once the Lord had fed the multitude on bread, since he

[12] Sermon 56.14, 15, 16, trans. Hill.

[13] *Sermon on the Mount* II, 9.30, 31, trans. Kavanagh.

> had believed that they would not have anything to eat (cf. John 6:7–13).[14]

It is surely very like our experience that we learn from our mistakes. So, in general terms, when we say, 'lead us not into temptation', we warn ourselves to ask not to be deprived of His help.[15]

In the sermons Augustine delivered to the candidates for baptism (teaching sermons) he goes into the question of temptation and sin more fully. In sermon 57 he writes:

> What was [God] teaching us? To fight against our covetous desires. It's true that in holy baptism you are going to shed your sins, but your desires remain which you've got to fight against. Conquer yourself and you've conquered the world.[16]

Then in Sermon 59 he writes:

> People are tempted in different ways; tempted with rewards, tempted with threats, if he (Satan) can't lead you astray by corrupting you, he tries to lead you astray by frightening you. But if you plant yourself firmly on God, and God hears you saying, 'Bring us not into temptation', then you overcome both evil love and vain fears. So, this too is something we need for this life, to ask not to be brought into temptation, because there are temptations here; and to be delivered from evil because evil is here.[17]

It would seem that self-knowledge and the recognition that some of our desires may be unworthy and that we need to try to reform them, are central tasks for Christians, and that the Lord's Prayer is a lifeline in our struggles to achieve those goals. To bring this into the everyday, what can we do in our daily lives as Christians?

Augustine mentions the desire for revenge more than once. Our ability or willingness to let revenge go raises the question, can we

---

[14] *Sermon on the Mount* II, 9.31, trans. Campbell.

[15] Letter 130 to Proba 12.21, translated in *Letters vol. 1 (1–82)*, trans. Sister Wilfrid Parsons SNB, The Fathers of the Church 12 (Catholic University of America, 1951).

[16] Sermon 57.9, trans. Hill.

[17] Sermon 59.8, trans. Hill.

forgive if the other person does not admit that they have wronged us? The answer must lie in Jesus's words on the Cross: 'Father, forgive them; for they do not know what they are doing' (Luke 23:34), and Stephen's as he was being stoned:'Lord, do not hold this sin against them.' (Acts 7:60).

The Lord's Prayer is not just about forgiveness, although Augustine emphasizes that time and again and must have realized how hard it would be for his listeners. It is a prayer in which we are allowed to ask for what we truly need, for ourselves and for others, and it allows us to think of the possibility that God's kingdom can come in us, and that we may be able to do His will now, not only in the life to come. Above all this prayer is addressed to the Father who is also Jesus's Father, and Jesus is alongside us as our brother as we pray. Augustine concludes Sermon 59:

> This prayer can be a great encouragement to you; in it you may not only learn to ask God your Father who is in heaven for whatever you desire, but also learn what you ought to desire.[18]

Tom Wright, following very much the same train of thought tells us that, 'In a sense, learning to follow Jesus is simply learning to pray the Lord's Prayer.'[19]

LONGER EXTRACTS FROM AUGUSTINE FOR FURTHER STUDY

Daily Bread

I agree, there are two ways of understanding this petition about daily bread, either with reference to our need for bodily victuals, or our need for spiritual nourishment. We obviously need material food for our daily victuals, and without it we can't live. Our needs include clothing, but we are to understand the whole from the part. When we ask for bread, we receive everything with it.

---

[18] Sermon 59.8, trans. Hill.

[19] Tom Wright, *God and the Pandemic: A Christian Reflection on the Coronavirus and its Aftermath* (SPCK, 2020), 19.

The faithful also know a spiritual sustenance, which you too are going to know, and to receive from the altar of God. That too will be a daily bread, necessary for this life. I mean, are we going to go on receiving the eucharist when we have come to Christ himself, and when we have begun to reign with him forever? So, the eucharist is our daily bread; but we should receive it in such a way that our minds and not just our bellies find refreshment. You see, the special property to be understood in it is unity, so that by being digested into his body and turned into his members we may be what we receive. Then it will really be our daily bread.

And the fact that I am dealing with this subject for you, and that you hear readings in the Church every day, is daily bread; and that you hear and sing hymns is daily bread. These are things we need on our pilgrimage.[20]

You ought to know what you have received, what you are going to receive, and what you ought to receive daily.[21]

Love of your Enemy

So now then, about these daily sins, for which I have told you that you have to say, as a kind of daily wash and brush up, 'Forgive us our debts, as we too forgive our debtors'—what are you going to do about them? You've got enemies; is there anyone living on this earth who doesn't have an enemy? Watch yourselves; love them—after all, what good do you get from things going wrong with your enemy? If he had nothing wrong with him, he wouldn't be your enemy. Wish him well, he stops being wrong, and he won't be an enemy. I mean it is not the human nature in him that is hostile to you, is it, but the fault in it. He is of the same stuff as you are, so we are brothers. You see, if your enemy dies, you are going without an enemy, I suppose, but you haven't found a

[20] Sermon 57.7, trans. Hill.

[21] Sermon 227 translated in *Sermons III/6 (184–229) on the Liturgical Seasons,* trans. Sister Mary Sarah Muldowney RSM, The Fathers of the Church 38 (Catholic University of America, 1959).

friend, but if it's his ill-nature that dies, then you have both lost an enemy and found a friend.[22]

Anger and Hatred

Forgive us our debts (Matt. 6:12), we say, and so we should, because we are saying the truth. Does anybody live in the flesh, and not have debts? Is there anybody living, for whom this prayer is not necessary? —Well, you know this from the creed you have given back, that among the other things you mentioned was the forgiveness of sins. There is one forgiveness of sins that is given only once; another that is given daily. There is one forgiveness of sins that is given only once in holy baptism; another which, as long as we live here, is given in the Lord's Prayer. That's why we say, *Forgive us our debts*.

And God has struck a bargain with us, an agreement and a definite contract, that we should say, *as we too forgive our debtors* (Matt. 6:12). If you want to say effectively, *Forgive us our debts*, you must say honestly, *as we too forgive our debtors*. If you don't say this second half, or say it dishonestly, then you say the first half in vain. I say to you above all, who are approaching holy baptism, forgive everything from the bottom of your hearts. And you, the faithful, who are using this occasion to hear this prayer and my commentary on it, forgive totally whatever you have against anybody from the bottom of your hearts; forgive precisely from the place into which God can see.

Sometimes a person forgives in words, and nurses a grudge in the heart; forgives in words because of other people, and nurses a grudge in the heart, quite unafraid of the eyes of God. Forgive absolutely; whatever grudges and grievances you have nursed up till these days, at least let go of them and forgive during these days. The sun ought not to have set upon your anger, and many suns have passed.

What is anger? Lust for revenge. What is hatred? Anger grown old. ... Anger is a speck, hatred a beam. Sometimes we rebuke someone for getting angry, and we are nursing hatred in our hearts; and

[22] Sermon 56.14, trans. Hill.

Christ says to us, *You see the speck in your brother's eye, and you do not see the beam in your own eye* (Luke 6.41). How has the speck managed to grow, to make a beam? Because it wasn't immediately plucked out. Because you allowed the sun to go out and come in so many times upon your anger, you made it old; you raked up evil suspicions, and you watered the speck, and by watering it you reared it, by rearing it you made it into a beam.

Amend your ways, straighten yourself out. If there were scorpions or vipers in your houses, what trouble you would go to in order to clear your houses of them, so that you could live in them without anxiety! You are always getting angry, and these rages grow old in your hearts, they turn into so many hates, so many beams, so many scorpions, so many snakes, and aren't you prepared to clear the house of God, your hearts, of these pests?

So do what it says, *as we too forgive our debtors*, and then say confidently, *Forgive us our debts*. But those great crimes, which it is good to have forgiven in baptism, and to which you should always be strangers, are one thing; quite another are daily sins without which one cannot live here, and because of which this daily prayer is so necessary—with its bargain, with its agreement—so that as you cheerfully say *Forgive us our debts*, you must also honestly say *as we too forgive our debtors*. Well, that is all we've got to say about past sins.[23]

Sister Susan SLG read Classics at Royal Holloway and taught for two years before joining the Community of the Sisters of the Love of God. In 2018 she was awarded an MA in Church History from the University of Nottingham. She is at present Garden Sister and Librarian at Fairacres Convent in Oxford.

[23] Sermon 58.6, 7, 8, trans. Hill.

The Holy Cross

Sister Rosemary SLG

On a hill far away stood an old rugged cross
The emblem of suffering and shame
And I love that old cross where the dearest and best
For a world of lost sinners was slain

Refrain: So I'll cherish the old rugged cross
Till my trophies at last I lay down
I will cling to the old rugged cross
And exchange it some day for a crown

O that old rugged cross, so despised by the world,
has a wondrous attraction for me; ...

In that old rugged cross, stained with blood so Divine,
a wondrous beauty I see, ...

To the old rugged cross I will ever be true ...

... I'll cherish the old rugged cross
Till my trophies at last I lay down
I will cling to the old rugged cross
And exchange it some day for a crown.

The Feast of the Holy Cross invites us to 'cherish' the Cross. We are to honour the Cross and its compelling beauty, blood-stained as it is, because of Him who died upon it, because of what happened there. On the feast day, the Cross is lifted up, placed in full view so that everyone can see it; so that we can look again at the Cross in case we have forgotten it. Look again in case, God forgive us, familiarity has bred contempt. In case the shocking things in the news have turned our stomachs, so that we want no more of anything like that, so gruesome, so frightening. The Crucified One has 'no form nor comeliness ... there is no beauty that we should desire him'

(Is. 53:2), unless we look with love and yield to the strange attraction of this Cross and what it stands for: the limitlessness of God's reconciling Love.

The Cross is there on every page of the New Testament. Its presence is implied, or referred to explicitly, in every text, and it reaches deep into our hearts: 'Do you not know that all of us who have been baptized into Christ Jesus were baptized into His death?' (Rom. 6:3) We have been signed with the Cross in Baptism and we make that sign often in a sweeping gesture which covers all that we are. By it we plunge into the mystery of the Father, the Son and the Holy Spirit, in a moment of recollection, as a blessing, a protection, a prayer, a thanksgiving, a witness; and an act of faith, obedience and love.

For the Sisters of the Love of God, Holy Cross day is particularly important because our Community was started on that day in 1906. Father Hollings SSJE, our Founder, maintained that the first Sisters were 'called into the wilderness for the sake of God'. So as wilderness people we can identify with the Israelites in Numbers 21, in the first reading at the Eucharist for the feast day, and try to understand that rather mystifying story: after the excitement of escape from Egypt, the wilderness turns out to be no joy ride or day trip. They have to go the long way round and make do with what the Lord provides. There is not enough, the food is terrible, who does he think they are to put up with it? They complain. Not too loudly, of course, but persistently. They murmur. And things go from bad to worse.

> Then the Lord sent poisonous serpents among the people, and they bit the people, so that many Israelites died. The people came to Moses and said, 'We have sinned by speaking against the Lord and against you; pray to the Lord to take away the serpents from us.' So Moses prayed for the people. And the Lord said to Moses, 'Make a poisonous serpent, and set it on a pole; and everyone who is bitten shall look at it and live.' (Num. 21:6–8)

What are we meant to understand by this? Does murmuring deserve a painful death? What was God doing? And what are we to make of it that the Evangelist cites the bronze serpent set up on a pole as a clue to the meaning of the Cross? Jesus says to Nicodemus:

> No one has ascended into heaven except the one who descended from heaven, the Son of Man. And just as Moses lifted up the serpent in the wilderness, so must the Son of Man be lifted up, that whoever believes in him may have eternal life. (John 3:13–15)

To dispel any disturbing suspicion that the people are healed because they worship the serpent, it helps to realize that the serpent is displayed as disabled, caught, so that it cannot reach the Israelites and they are safe from its poisonous bite. But we need to go deeper. What is displayed in the story is God's anger at the murmuring of the people, showing that their lack of faith in God's care is not a trivial matter and it has consequences. With hindsight we can read His anger as an indication of how much He is hurt. God cares. He cannot help caring because His fundamental nature is outgoing love.

The shock of the death-dealing serpents works: the people move from murmuring to an appeal to Moses for help, and Moses does help them: he appeals to God on their behalf. God responds: the serpent lifted up on a pole proclaims that the people's relationship with God, once dislocated by their lack of faith, has been restored. To realize this they must *look,* and *see,* and be healed: 'whoever *believes* in Him may have eternal life'.

> My eyes are ever towards the Lord: for he shall pluck my feet out of the net. (Ps. 25:15)
>
> The eye of the Lord is upon them that fear him: on those who trust in his mercy. (Ps 33:18)

Such looking in faith and being seen does not suddenly, magically, make everything all right. We are still in snake country, serpent country, like Adam and Eve. But evil now is fatally disabled and made ultimately powerless.

George Bennard, who wrote 'The old rugged Cross' did not write the hymn all at once. It happened that he preached at a revivalist meeting and his testimony was mocked by a group of youths. Upset and humiliated by this, he sought comfort in the Cross. Then the tune, with no words, came to him. And, gradually, some words as well. Only months later did he compose the subsequent verses, it became a hymn which others could sing too and was a great hit.[1] I think I must have heard it on the wireless in the 1950s 'with Sandy MacPherson on the organ'! It must have lodged somewhere inside me and, on occasion, it has seen me through a difficult time.

Contemplative seeing comes slowly too. As we draw near to the Cross of Jesus, we can expect to feel our deepest needs at a point where they touch the world's wound. We may wish to flee. Jesus himself, when His hour had come and He faced the Cross head-on, wanted to be let off. He was not let off and He did not flee; He gave full consent to the Father's loving will. His priestly prayer, in John 17, tells us something of what was in His heart. He, pure in heart, undistracted by self-concerns, could see, even at that moment, God; and God's purposes at work.

> My eyes are ever towards the Lord: for he shall pluck my feet out of the net.
>
> The eye of the Lord is upon them that fear him: on those who trust in his mercy.

The Cross is *holy* because it takes us into God. It is a sign because it points beyond itself. The meanings attached to the Cross have multiplied over the centuries in writings of great beauty and power, sometimes indeed over-thought, decorating it, and thereby obscuring it. But the starkness remains. Father Cary taught the Sisters that they would learn more in their silent hours of prayer before the crucifix than in the pages of the newspapers. Father Gilbert wrote in his *Pilgrim's Book of Prayers*:

> Resolve therefore to meditate often and long upon Christ's Passion and his suffering love. He will never let us go if we really want to stay with him. ... So we may bring its reality to bear upon the passing circumstances of the world in which we are called to live and work for him. ... Calvary reaches out to the very limits of being human, to the very bounds of creation.[2]

---

[1] George W. Sanville, 'The Old Rugged Cross', in *Forty Gospel Hymn Stories* (Rodeheaver-Hall Mack, 1943), 16.

[2] Gilbert Shaw, *A Pilgrim's Book of Prayers* (A. R. Mowbray, 1945; repr. SLG Press, 1970), 99 and 95.

The Cross is holy; the Cross is a sign. The Cross is a gift in that it requires only our empty-handedness and willingness to receive. We pray that we may be faithful to the Cross, and give thanks to God who so cherishes us.

Sister Rosemary SLG entered the Community of the Sisters of the Love of God in 1971.

How to Live with the Passions: An Ancient Approach to Human Frailty by Maximus the Confessor

Bronwen Neil

The term 'passion' in the Byzantine monastic tradition is often used as the equivalent of vice. It 'nearly always indicates something evil'.[1] Monastic discussions of the passions, such as those found in the *Sayings of the Desert Fathers*, reveal an awareness of the huge variety of personality types, and that each required different approaches by those who mentored their spiritual practice.[2]

Maximus the Confessor (580–662 AD) is perhaps the greatest synthesizer of the Byzantine tradition on the spiritual life. His spiritual psychology is centred on the single concept of love: how we relate to God, to our neighbour, to ourselves, and to the natural world. Several of his texts focus on how to live out these relationships in a practical way. These include his *Centuries on Love*, in 400 short paragraphs, and the *Centuries on Theology and the Incarnate Dispensation of the Son of God*.[3] He also penned two *Books of Difficulties* (*Ambigua*)

---

[1] Andrew Louth, *Maximus the Confessor*, Early Christian Fathers (Routledge, 1996), 41. This book introduces various key texts on the spiritual life with translations. I have used my own translations, unless otherwise noted. Translations from other authors have been adjusted to be gender inclusive.

[2] Louth, *Maximus*, 37. For one of the first translations of the Sayings into English, see Benedicta Ward SLG, *Apophthegmata Patrum* as *The Sayings of the Desert Fathers: The Alphabetical Collection*, Revised edition (Liturgical Press, 1984) and the *Lives* of the desert mothers in *Harlots of the Desert* (Liturgical Press, 1987).

[3] *Centuries on Love*, trans. in G. Berthold, *Maximus Confessor: Selected Writings*, Classics of Western Spirituality (Paulist Press, 1985), 35–98; *Centuries on Theology and the Incarnate Dispensation of the Son of God*, trans. in Luis Joshua Salés, *Two Hundred Chapters on Theology*, Popular Patristics Series 53 (St Vladimir's Seminary Press, 2015).

on difficult passages of Scripture and several letters pertaining to this subject, especially the *Letter to Thalassius*.[4] For Maximus, love is the absolutely universal relationship and, as Louth puts it, 'training in Christian spiritual practice amounts to a training in love'.[5] Maximus's contribution is significant for a contemporary Christian understanding of the value of emotional detachment from the passions. It offers an interesting contrast to modern psychological theories of personality types and their characterization by particular passions or weaknesses.

Maximus defined passion as 'the impulse of the soul contrary to nature', which Andrew Louth glossed as 'moods or desires that come upon us, often obsessively, and disturb or distract us'.[6] Maximus's examples include an irrational love for food or wealth or any material thing or a woman (or man) or any passing glory. The opposite of passion is dispassion (*apatheia*), and this was seen as the goal of the ascetic struggle by Greek, Palestinian, Syrian and Egyptian monks as well as those in the West who, like Augustine, were influenced by neo-Platonism. The neo-Platonic ascent to God was seen to take place in three stages: (i) the ascetic struggle and purification of the body; (ii) meditation, or spiritual contemplation of the natural world; and (iii) prayer, or divine contemplation. These stages were not mutually exclusive or sequential: one could make progress on one level and fall behind on another. The final stage, of divine contemplation, was not so much a stage as an end goal, only to be achieved perfectly in the afterlife. I will examine how Maximus viewed the role of the passions in each of these stages of the spiritual life.

The main influence on Maximus's theory of the passions, with some adaptation, was Evagrius of Pontus (*d.* 399 AD), a Greek monk who wrote various treatises on the ascetical life for monks in the

[4] *Letter to Thalassius* and selected texts from the *Ambigua*, trans. in P. Blowers and Robert Louis Wilken, *On the Cosmic Mystery of Jesus Christ: St Maximus the Confessor*, Popular Patristics Series 25 (St Vladimir's Seminary Press, 2003).

[5] Louth, *Maximus*, 38.

[6] *Centuries on Love*, II.16, Louth, *Maximus*, 36.

Egyptian desert, such as *The Practical Treatise*, also known simply as *The Monk*, and the *Gnostic Centuries* (*Kephalaia Gnostica*).[7] Maximus's other influences include Nemesius of Emesa, a fourth- to fifth-century writer in Syria.[8] All of these writers worked and thought within a neo-Platonic framework in which they sought to develop a distinctively Christian view of the spiritual life as lived in community. I will consider some of the features of Maximus's teaching on the passions that can be traced to these sources, while pointing to several key differences between Maximus and Evagrius on this subject. Finally, I examine the three phases of learning to live with the passions, according to Maximus.

Understanding the Passions

Maximus and Evagrius both distinguished between bodily passions, such as hunger, thirst and lust, and passions of the soul. The bodily passions do not concern us here. The passions of the soul which are problematic are those which are 'contrary to nature', not those passions which are natural.[9] The natural passions, or those which were in accordance with human nature before the Fall, are perfectly appropriate if directed towards God. These include things like hunger, thirst, and the desire for sleep. According to Evagrius the eight principal 'unnatural' passions of the soul were gluttony, fornication, avarice, grief, anger, accidie (i.e. listlessness), vainglory and pride. Maximus adopted these eight principal passions from Evagrius with some revisions: there is no equivalent to Evagrian grief, Maximus replaced it with fear; vainglory and pride have been reduced to the single passion of pride;

---

[7] *Evagrius of Pontus: The Greek Ascetic Corpus*, trans. with introd. Robert E. Sinkewicz (Oxford University Press, 2003); *Kephalaia Gnostica*, ed. in M. W. Frankenburg, *Evagrius Ponticus* (Weidmann, 1912).

[8] Nemesius was the author of a treatise *Περὶ φύσεως ἀνθρώπου*, or *De natura hominis* ('On Human Nature'), trans. in *Nemesius On the Nature of Man*, trans. and introd. by Philip van der Eijk & R.W. Sharples, Translated Texts for Historians (Liverpool University Press, 2008).

[9] *Centuries on Love*, II.16, Louth, *Maximus*, 47.

Maximus gave a prominent place to passions with social consequences such as resentment and envy, which Evagrius either ignores or subsumes into others.[10]

Following Plato's three-part division of the soul, Maximus explained how each part was affected by particular passions in *Ambigua* X.44. The taxonomy of the soul in this passage borrows heavily from the neo-Platonist Nemesius of Emesa's *On Human Nature.*[11] Writing in the fourth century BC, Plato had divided the soul into three parts: first and highest in his scheme was the rational mind; second came the irrational incensive (or irascible) part; third, the irrational desiring (or concupiscent) part. The rational part of the soul was affected most by the passions of vainglory and pride.[12] The irascible part, the source of the soul's energy, was affected particularly by grief and anger. The desiring part was affected by gluttony, fornication, and avarice. All three were affected by accidie or listlessness.

For neo-Platonists like Evagrius, Nemesius and Maximus, there were two elements of the passionate part of the soul controlling and disordering our emotions. These were the incensive faculty, that is, the source of the soul's energy, and the desiring faculty of the soul. The passions linked the soul to the physical world. When the intellect was filled with God, the passion of irascibility would be transformed into Divine Love, and desire would be changed into intense longing for God.[13] That is why Maximus can write of 'the blessed passion of holy love' as our goal, through the transformation of the irascible and the desiring faculties of the soul.[14]

---

[10] *Centuries on Love,* III.90–1, Louth, *Maximus,* 39.

[11] Nemesius of Emesa, *On the Nature of Man,* trans. R. W. Sharples and P. J. van der Eijk (Liverpool University Press, 2008).

[12] *Ad Thalassium,* 64, in *Quaestiones ad Thalassium,* eds. C. Laga and C. Steel, Corpus Christianorum Series Graeca 22 (Brepols, 1990), 221; trans. Blowers and Wilken, 162.

[13] *Centuries on Love,* III.56 and II.48.

[14] *Centuries on Love,* III.67, cited by Louth, *Maximus,* 40–1.

Evagrius's and Maximus's Theories of the Passions

While Maximus clearly owed a great debt to Evagrius, a number of crucial differences can be identified in his theory of the passions.[15] Three of these differences stand out as noteworthy.

1. Conquering the passions in communities of believers.

Evagrius's doctrine of prayer and the spiritual life was intended to enable the soul 'to regain the state of being a pure mind from which it has fallen',[16] but for Maximus, the spiritual life was about how we love in community. Maximus believed that it was easier to conquer the passions in communities, not hermitages. The passions for Evagrius were simply a register of the state of the soul, and were thus only of interest to the individual in their quest for enlightenment. Maximus, however, saw the passions as the product of relationships with others.[17] It is easy to be dispassionate when you are alone on a mountaintop! Maximus emphasized love expressed in relationship rather than a solitary intellectual pursuit of the Divine. The spiritual disciple needs a guide or teacher because dispassion can lead to the passions of vainglory and pride, to which the only antidote is humility, expressed in obedience to a spiritual father or mother.

Unlike Evagrius, Maximus did not accept the dualistic doctrine of Origen of Alexandria (*c.* 185–*c.* 253) concerning the relationship between our body and our soul. Evagrius had accepted Origen's theory of embodiment as a punishment, stating that 'Movement [of the soul] is the cause of evil.'[18] Maximus described a different order of events in the soul's progress towards God, starting with the soul's birth into a body, followed by its movement towards God, and culminating in

[15] A classic study of the impact of Evagrius on Maximus's spiritual theology is M. Viller, 'Aux sources de la spiritualité de S. Maxime: les œuvres d'Évagre le Pontique', *Revue d'ascétique et de mystique*, 11 (1930), 156–84, 239–68, 331–6.

[16] Louth, *Maximus*, 38.

[17] Louth, *Maximus*, 39.

[18] *Kephalaia Gnostica*, I.51.

the soul finding rest in God.[19] Thus, according to Maximus, movement of the soul was not evil in itself, and could be directed by reason:

> The soul moves according to reason when the concupiscent part is ruled by self-restraint, when the irascible part turns away from sin and attains to charity, and when reason directs itself to God through prayer and spiritual knowledge.[20]

Maximus's belief in the possibility for personal transformation in this life is rather different from the typical Western emphasis of Ambrose, Augustine, Jerome and others, on the notion of the essential flaw in our natures caused by original sin that will prevent us from being united with God if we are not redeemed through baptism. Maximus's emphasis is rather on restored human nature, which was the purpose and consequence of the incarnation of Christ in human form. As Maximus put it:

> For it was necessary, necessary in truth, for him to become the light unto that earth ... so that ... he might wondrously liberate human nature from its bondage to these things under the Evil One, and endow it with the inextinguishable light of true knowledge and the indefatigable power of the virtues.[21]

His focus is not on human corruption but incorruption, which is first received when the Christian is baptized in Christ through the Spirit.[22]

2. Passions are neutral in themselves.

In Evagrius, the passions were points of attack for demons and had to be transcended; for Maximus, however, they were neutral in themselves and could be transformed into vices (those which are contrary to our pre-fallen nature) or virtues (those in conformity with our pre-fallen nature).[23] While Evagrius identified the two causes of evil as bad thoughts inspired by demons and evil thoughts inspired by our

[19] Discussed by Paul Blowers in *On the Cosmic Mystery*, 24–7.
[20] *Centuries on Love*, IV.15.
[21] *Ad Thalassium*, 64, ed. Laga and Steel, 197; trans. Blowers and Wilken, 150.
[22] *Centuries on Theology and the Incarnate Dispensation*, I.87.
[23] Viller, 'Aux sources', 181.

fallen will, Maximus identified three causes of evil: demons, the fallen will, and the passions.[24] The fallen will did not accord with our natural will, that which is in conformity with God's will for us.[25]

3. The power of obsessive thoughts leads to passions.

Whereas Evagrius used the notions of an obsessive chain of thought (*logismos*) and passion interchangeably,[26] for Maximus obsessive thoughts were the precursors to a passion. So, for example, debilitating sexual desire would be an obsessive thought, while fornication would be the passion resulting from putting this thought into action. For a monk or nun, any degree of sexual desire was seen as inappropriate, while for a non-celibate lay person, lust was regarded as a normal bodily passion. The passions had to be removed first, before one could deal with obsessive thoughts. When one's thoughts became 'mere thoughts' and did not incite the passions, the highest state of dispassion had been reached.

Not all obsessive chains of thought *(logismoi)* were intrinsically evil, however. There were also natural ones worthy of the soul engaged in contemplating and knowing divine mysteries: such was the passion of holy love, as we shall see.[27]

The Threefold Path to God

Now that we appreciate how Maximus understood the passions, we can consider their role in the Christian's three-fold path to God. As I have noted, in Maximus's writings, as in those of Evagrius, the struggle with the passions took place in the first of three stages of ascent to God. Progress from one stage to the next was not linear

---

[24] *Centuries on Love*, II.33 and III.93, cited by Viller, 'Aux sources', 180 & n. 97.

[25] For further discussion of Maximus's view of the vices and virtues and the workings of the will, see *The Oxford Companion to Maximus the Confessor*, ed. Pauline Allen and Bronwen Neil (Oxford University Press, 2015).

[26] Viller, 'Aux sources', 181 n. 102.

[27] *Ad Thalassium*, 64, ed. Laga and Steel, 211; trans. Blowers and Wilken, 156 and 157 n. 8.

nor sequential, but allowed for overlap and regression in the disciple's journey. We have seen that the three neo-Platonic phases of this journey are ascetic struggle, meditation on rational and spiritual principles, and divine contemplation.

Stage 1. Ascetic Struggle: Purification of the Body.

While Evagrius saw the ascetic struggle as the special province of the solitary monk or nun, Maximus had a more inclusive notion of it as necessary for anyone who sought to develop their spiritual nature. The aim of the ascetic struggle was apatheia, or dispassion. This is an unusual noun in English, but the associated adjective, 'dispassionate', is commonly used. Apatheia could also be translated as 'impassibility'. It was the state of detachment from the irrational parts of the soul but it was not detachment for its own sake, 'but only so that, in their purified state, they can be reintegrated into the whole human being'.[28] Only through such reintegration could Christians fully and truly love God, and consequently love themselves (as made in the image of God) and the rest of the created world. Trying to love God with only part of the soul was doomed to fail.

The sequence of virtues that led to dispassion followed each other like links in a chain, starting with the fundamental link of faith. Faith led to fear of God, which led to complete self-control, which in turn produced patience and forbearance. Patience and forbearance generated hope in God, which led to dispassion and ultimately to love.[29] What Maximus meant by dispassion was not merely disinterestedness, which would be a very solitary virtue, but also a 'purified love' that could only be manifested in relationships with other people, with ourselves and ultimately with God.[30] The path from being mastered by the passions to being able to control them without disturbance of the soul was the path of personal development from self-love or egotism, the mother of the passions,

[28] Louth, *Maximus*, 41.

[29] *Centuries on Love*, I.1–2, cited by Louth, *Maximus*, 38.

[30] Louth, *Maximus*, 41.

to love of others. The fulfilment of scriptural law consisted in the mutual union of love:

> And if their ethical conduct and way of life are the same, they clearly also share the same bond of judgment in their relation to each other, a bond which guides them in single-mindedness toward the one principle of human nature, in which there is absolutely none of the divisions that possesses human nature because of self-love ... By this love [of others], in turn, the scriptural law reaches its true fulfilment as all human beings are joined to one another in mutual love.[31]

The ultimate test of dispassion was being able to show love to one's enemies.[32] This was only possible through detachment from the passions, especially those with communal impact such as hatred, grief, anger and resentment. The state of dispassion was not passive but active. Its outcome was virtue which, with practice, could become a habit of mind.

Stage 2. Meditation: Freeing the Mind from the Passions.

Dispassion leads to 'mere thoughts', which signal 'the beginnings of natural contemplation'.[33] Mere thoughts are those that are free from passion, like the thoughts that are allowed to rise up and pass away without judgement in Buddhist meditation. As Maximus writes in *Centuries on Love*:

> If the thoughts that continually rise up in the heart are free from passion, whether the body is awake or asleep, then we may know that we have attained the highest state of dispassion.[34]

These are thoughts purified, having transcended self-love. Louth notes:

> 'Mere thoughts', then, for Maximus are a sign of that detachment that enables us to engage in the world and with others in a non-possessive way—with respect.[35]

---

[31] *Ad Thalassium,* 64, ed. Laga and Steel, 235, trans. Blowers and Wilken, 168.

[32] *Centuries on Love,* I.61, cited by Louth, *Maximus,* 39–40.

[33] Louth, *Maximus,* 42.

[34] *Centuries on Love,* I.93.

[35] Louth, *Maximus,* 42.

Once the mind has been freed from the passions, it can engage without distraction in meditation or contemplation of the natural order. This involves a lot more than appreciation of the natural world. It is rather the contemplation of the rational principles that underpin the natural order.

The concept of *logoi* (the plural of *logos*) comes from Origen: they are the principles according to which the Logos, meaning Christ the Word of God, created everything in the cosmos.[36] *Logoi* are the inner meanings in things. According to Maximus, the Fall has obscured our vision:

> we tend not to see God's meaning in the world and all its parts, rather we tend to see the world in relation to ourselves and read into it our meaning.[37]

We have created an I-centred universe. Learning to see creation as God sees it, or seeing the principles in the natural order, amounts to much the same thing as the Theravada Buddhist notion of insight (*vipassana*). It is seeing things as they really are, and also seeing each other as created in the Image of God. Much interpersonal conflict arises from different perceptions of reality. Being freed from private prejudices and judgements created by the passions is learning to manage our personality. It means accepting reality as it is and not as we would like it to be. The outcome of this stage is knowledge: knowledge of incorporeal beings and corporeal beings, or knowledge of the Logos, the Word of God, at work in the world.

Stage 3. Divine Contemplation: Union with God in Prayer.

The third stage is that of prayer or divine contemplation. Prayer is a state rather than an activity.[38] Evagrius put it beautifully when he described prayer as 'the state of the soul illuminated solely by the light of the Holy Trinity in ecstasy'.[39] This is the state of spiritual perfection;

---

[36] Louth, *Maximus*, 37.

[37] Ibid.

[38] Ibid.

[39] Evagrius, *Kephalaia Gnostica*, VII.29, ed. Frankenberg, 452, cited by Viller, 'Aux sources', 251.

the irrational parts of the soul are not rejected but redirected: desire is transformed into divine eros, and irascibility is transformed into love for the Divine.[40] Thus both desire and anger are reintegrated and the soul can love God in its completeness.

This third and final stage is a matter of experience, not of intellectual speculation. Here Maximus adopts the teaching of Pseudo-Dionysius the Areopagite (*fl. c.* 600) on apophatic union, the ineffable loss of self in the Divine. After the initial stages of affirming what we know about God and then denying that which we affirmed we could know about God, we reach the stage of union which is beyond words. Our final union with God is the union of unknowing, when the intellect is taken outside itself in ecstatic love for God. This is the state of pure prayer. As Maximus puts it, '(s)he who truly loves God prays entirely without distraction, and (s)he who prays entirely without distraction loves God truly'.[41] The outcome of this stage is wisdom, the wisdom of the knowledge of God, in so far as that is possible for human beings.[42] Such wisdom is accompanied by joy:

> when a person is perfected in wisdom, (s)he acquires unspeakable joy, a potent joy able to maintain that person with a godly and divine sustenance.[43]

To provide a concrete example from scripture, Maximus gives an interpretation of the story of Jonah, in which Jonah is a figure of the passions of humanity. Jonah's progress is described as a descent from Joppa, signifying virtue, knowledge, and the wisdom that is based on both of those gifts, to the sea, understood as the abyss of human nature's slavery to ignorance and evil.[44]

---

[40] *Centuries on Love*, II.48.
[41] Idem, II.1, cited by Louth, *Maximus*, 38.
[42] Idem, II.26.
[43] *Ad Thalassium*, 64, ed. Laga and Steel, 189; trans. Blowers and Wilken, 147.
[44] Idem, 147–9.

Conclusion

Ascetical theology can, at times, seem negative, focussing on cutting off the passions and separating oneself from the world. Maximus provided a significant corrective to this view, by balancing this negative side of the spiritual struggle with a positive emphasis on the importance of pure and deeper love. His whole theology of the passions can be summarized in one quotation from the *Centuries on Love*: 'A pure soul is one freed from passions and consequently delighted by divine love.'[45] This love is directed not towards the self, but towards God and others.

Unlike those who followed Origen of Alexandria's teaching on what was needed to free the soul from passions, Maximus believed that it is not enough for a Christian to achieve freedom from the passions and gain a purely intellectual attachment to the truth and Divine Knowledge. Freeing the soul from passions was not about the individual attaining a disembodied pure mind, and it was more easily attained in community than in hermitages. For Maximus, the spiritual life must be practised in a community at least of two persons, namely the disciple and a spiritual mother or father.[46] The three phases of purification of the body, meditation to free the mind from the passions, and spiritual union with God, were more easily achievable in community than by an individual in isolation.

Ascetical theology is all about how we come to know God. For Maximus, to know God is to love God, and to be deified through the Holy Spirit by grace. Deification is the purpose and consequence of the incarnation, which restored the original harmony and wholeness of the cosmos. There is thus an important place for the passions in the Christian path towards union with God. This is an original and cautiously optimistic theology of the passions as part of the Christian life, and one which takes cognizance of individual weaknesses and the danger of obsessive thoughts. It offers a practical goal for achieving harmony within ourselves and harmony with others in

[45] *Centuries on Love*, I.34.

[46] Idem, III.66.

community. Maximus's teaching on the passion of holy love thereby makes a valuable contribution and corrective to modern Western conceptions of spiritual development which often tend to focus on the individual personality, rather than on the person as member of a faith community.

Bronwen Neil is Professor of Ancient History and teaches Latin and Byzantine history in the Department of History and Archaeology at Macquarie University, Sydney, and Fellow of the Australian Academy of Humanities. She completed her PhD at Australian Catholic University in 1999 in the Centre for Early Christian Studies. She joined Macquarie University as Professor of Ancient History in 2017. She is co-author with Prof. Pauline Allen of three books on Maximus the Confessor and his life, and co-editor of the *Oxford Handbook of Maximus the Confessor* (Oxford University Press, 2015), co-author of *Greek and Latin Letters in Late Antiquity* (Cambridge University Press, 2020), and the author of *Dreams and Divination from Byzantium to Baghdad (400–1000 CE)* (Oxford University Press, 2021).

SSJE, SLG and the Heart

Sister Clare-Louise SLG

SLG and the Sacred Heart

The Sisters of the Love of God are not known for their devotions: we have never had a set of Stations of the Cross in our Chapels, had statues other than that of Our Lady, or had Benediction; we do not own a monstrance. So, on the face of it there is no particular devotion to the Sacred Heart. In fact, many of us may be actively 'turned off' by the traditional Sacred Heart imagery of the bleeding heart exposed on Jesus's breast (Llangasty actually has a very tasteful one).

Having said that it does not mean that we do not have a devotional aspect to our lives, individual or corporate. Our names of dedication are one proof of that. Carmelite friars and nuns often take names of dedication, and perhaps the tradition may have come to SLG through that. As Sisters we may consider our own dedication: is it a forgotten part of our names? Might it be time to reflect on it again, and how that might affect each of our lives as an individual before God? Father Cary's Rule told the Sisters that they should use their own particular names of dedication

> ... as a means towards realizing the claim of the personal love of Jesus of which their consecrated chastity is a recognition.[1]

Our dedications come from some particular aspect or mystery of Christ towards which a Sister feels a calling; this becomes in some way part of her being. I think it was Sister Barbara June who said that she sometimes 'borrowed' another Sister's dedication when it gave her pause for thought on her own spiritual journey. Although few of us have had dedications to the Sacred Heart over the years, the Heart of God, as the expression of His love for us, lies beneath them all.

---

[1] Father Cary's Rule, chapter 9, 'Chastity'.

I will return to that idea of 'realizing the claim of the personal love of Jesus' from Father Cary's Rule later, but first I want to reflect on the influence of the spirituality of the Society of St John the Evangelist on our earliest Sisters.

Father Richard Meux Benson (1824–1915) was founder of the Cowley Fathers and one of the prominent figures in the Oxford Movement at the end of the nineteenth and beginning of the twentieth centuries. Christ Church College gave him the country living of St James and St Francis, Cowley, then a small village two and a half miles from Oxford, with a parish that extended to Magdalen Bridge.

For nine years Benson, who was described as 'an embodiment of the devotion, reserve, austerity and self-effacement of the Tractarians', lived in Cowley in prayer and labour among the poor.[2] He felt a call to missionary work and had set his heart on working in India but, at the last moment, when he was on the point of leaving England, Samuel Wilberforce, then Bishop of Oxford, begged him to remain and deal with the large new suburb of Oxford which was growing up on the Cowley side of Magdalen Bridge, in the newly developing area of East Oxford.[3] Benson arranged the construction of the Iron Church in Stockmore Street which was opened on 19 October 1859, dedicated to St John the Evangelist. This was the precursor to the Church of St Mary and St John on the Cowley Road, to which the congregation moved in 1883. In 1866, Father Benson founded the Society of St John the Evangelist and in 1869 he became the first vicar of the Parish of Cowley St John: 'Father Benson preached regularly and his sermons, packed with knowledge, could last as much as three hours'.[4]

---

[2] From the *Project Canterbury* website, 'Richard Meux Benson' at anglicanhistory.org/ bios/benson.html, accessed 23 November 2023.

[3] Benson was eventually able to fulfil his desire for missionary work in India after he stood down as superior of the Society of St John the Evangelist in 1890.

[4] From the website of the Parish of Cowley St John Churchyard, Oxford, 'Fact Sheet 2, Father Richard Meux Benson', at www.ssmjchurchyard.org.uk/ father_benson.php, accessed 23 November 2023.

As mission priests, the Society of St John the Evangelist combined prayer with parish work and social action. In Cowley Father Benson was involved in the foundation of schools, the Gladiator, a working men's club, and the All Saints Home for Incurables (now St John's Home).

As befits a Community dedicated to St John the Evangelist, the Beloved Disciple, the priests and brothers of the Community had a strong devotional sense of the humanity of Jesus. Like their patron they leaned on the breast of their Lord, and their homilies and retreat addresses reflect what Father Cary called the Mysteries of Incarnate Love.

One of the things that strikes me is the link the Society embodied between dedicated lives of prayer and committed work among the poorest members of their parishes.

We see this also in Father Gilbert Shaw in Poplar: both he and Father Cary saw a need for Communities of prayer, whose work was intimately connected to and supported through prayer. This was not about groups of men and women retiring for a quiet life of undisturbed prayer and reflection. The Fathers of SSJE and Father Gilbert believed contemplative communities were intimately connected with the struggle to help those in need, through costly spiritual work on their behalf.

Reflecting on the early teaching of these nineteenth-century Fathers we get a sense of the deep commitment to, and love of, the Lord Jesus, that was central to their lives and was the wellspring of their mission. In 1868, in a retreat given to the All Saints Sisters of the Poor, Father Benson said:

> We must go forth into the world with a heart which imitates the Heart of Jesus. It is for us to have that Heart really communicated to us; it is for us to ask Gim to take our hearts away and give us His—that Heart which He yearns to find reproduced.[5]

---

[5] Granville Mercer Williams SSJE, *Look to the Glory: an anthology taken from the writings and from notes made at retreats of the Reverend Richard Meux Benson* (SSJE, 1966), 30. (1966 was the Society's centenary year.)

Here we return more specifically to the theme of the Sacred Heart: for the brethren of SSJE, the Sacred Heart was the locus of the love of God for His world, and dwelling in His heart of love was the source of their lives of missionary service.

Where did the Brethren (and later SLG) go, to gain that sort of a heart? In an SSJE Community Retreat that was given in 1875 Father Benson said:

> Dwell in the Heart of Jesus. Read the mysteries of Love which can only be found in that sacred enclosure; as thou goest on thy way let this be the power of all thy actions, so He will make Thee to triumph.[6]

In another address he stipulated:

> The Religious is separated from all in order that he may be identified with all. He is separated from all, but he is gathered into the Heart of Jesus Christ which encloses all. Living in the Heart of Jesus, he must find all worldly associations transfigured, glorified.[7]

Here we can see where 'devotion to the Sacred Heart' can find its place in our own lives. I quoted above from Father Cary's Rule which told us to realize 'the claim of the personal love of Jesus' through our personal names of dedication. As Father Hollings Rule stated many years earlier:

> To this great grace of humility we shall attain as we obey Our Lord's command, 'Learn of Me, for I am meek and lowly of heart', and because the heart that so learns becomes as the very Heart of Jesus, it shall truly know Him.[8]

Father Cary's teaching on the Sacred Heart was given in retreats on the subject in the period leading up to the Second World War, before he was our Father Director. The *Anima Christi* retreat was given to SLG in 1932 and the *Veni Creator Spiritus* retreat given to a different group of SLG in 1937. The records of the retreats are handwritten,

---

[6] Williams, *Look to the Glory*, 31.

[7] Idem, 31–2.

[8] Father Hollings's Rule, Chapter 2, 'Of Mental Prayer'.

and I focussed on the *Anima Christi* retreat. In this retreat Father Cary used the following headings, which give a flavour of the direction of his thought:

- The Sacred Heart as the Throne of Divine Perfection.
- The Sacred Heart as the Temple and Throne of the Holy Spirit.
- The Sacred Heart as the Refuge of Sinners.
- The Sacred Heart as the School of Prayer (looking at the example of Our Lord in His relationship with His Father as a pattern of prayer).
- The Eucharistic Heart of Jesus (as the primary place to meet the Love of God).

He also spoke specifically about intimacy with the Sacred Heart:

> We find our way of access to the Heart of Jesus most truly in our intensive life of prayer. That is what is procured for us in so far as we have entered in any way whatever upon a life of contemplation, through bringing the Sacred Humanity of Jesus into the forefront of our life ... it is in the Heart of Jesus, Jesus as He is in His Glory, that we find set before us the vision of the Life and Love of God ... there is no short-cut to this intimacy with the sacred Heart. ... It is here in this kind of intimacy with the Heart of Jesus, this most holy state where the Precious Blood does its most perfect work within the ransomed life, that there is found that Christ-like perception of the needs and sorrows of the world which He has ransomed, and of the character and power of the Love of God to Whom we are redeemed.

What can we draw out from this for ourselves? The final section of that quotation, where Father Cary links intimacy with Christ with 'a Christ-like perception of the needs and sorrows of the world', is perhaps the first thing to consider. To see the 'needs and sorrows of the world' as Christ does, is to enter into—as our 'Way of Life' puts it—'the Love behind the Passion'.

Father Cary also talks about 'bringing the Sacred Humanity of Jesus into the forefront of our lives'. Teresa of Avila in the *Book of Her Life* recounts her experience of 'learned men' telling her 'to rid [herself] of all corporeal images'—even that of the Incarnate Lord—

'to attain perfect contemplation'.[9] Teresa tried to follow this advice, but soon found it to be a mistake, at least in her experience. She tells us that when God leads us into higher states of prayer, the presence of the Incarnate Jesus may seem to disappear. But when we try to force that experience, perhaps in an attempt to attain the silent undistracted prayer that we think we should be enjoying, Teresa tells us very firmly:

> The soul is left floating in the air, as they say; it seems it has no support no matter how much it may think it is full of God.[10]

The Cowley Fathers placed great emphasis and reflection on the various mysteries of Christ, including the Sacred Heart, and what better way of drawing near to God than reflection on these mysteries. As Teresa says, that does not mean long and lengthy reflections, it means a steadfast gaze of love:

> Represent the Lord Himself as close to you and behold how lovingly and humbly He is teaching you. ... I'm not asking you now that you think about Him, or that you draw out a lot of concepts or make long and subtle reflections with your intellect. I'm not asking you to do anything more than look at Him. For who can keep you from turning your eyes towards this Lord, even if you do so just for a moment if you can't do more?[11]

Teresa is inviting us to adopt a very simple gaze of love, sometimes with the help of an icon, crucifix or candle; a directing of our attention. Teresa complained that she was not able to make the complicated imaginations suggested by Ignatian spirituality: her mind just would not do it. But if we cannot construct visual meditations, what are we to do in order to remain in the presence of God?

---

[9] *The Book of Her Life*, chapter 22, para. 1, trans. in Kieran Kavanaugh OCD, Otilio Rodriguez OCD, *The Collected Works of St. Teresa of Avila*, vol. 1 (Institute of Carmelite Studies, 1976), 195.

[10] *The Book of Her Life*, chapter 22, para. 9.

[11] *The Way of Perfection*, chapter 26, paras. 1 and 3, trans. Kieran Kavanaugh OCD, Otilio Rodriguez OCD, *The Collected Works of St. Teresa of Avila*, vol. 2 (Institute of Carmelite Studies, 1976), 133.

We all have our own ways of doing this, but the Sacred Heart can become more than a concept: it can become our home, where we habitually dwell, through a simple 'gaze' of love. It stops us from 'floating in the air' to use Teresa's phrase, and grounds us in the incarnate life of our Blessed Lord; in His love and mercy revealed so much by His heart. As Sister Susan described in her examination of the words of the Our Father, Jesus becomes our brother and our friend, our lover and our companion. Rather than trying to reach the heights of contemplation through our own abilities, like a child or like the Beloved Disciple, we rest on the heart of Jesus.

The Heart in Prayer.

The second part of this reflection focusses on the heart in prayer, or the prayer of the heart. When I considered the idea of the Sacred Heart this is where my own mind immediately went as a concept and a devotion with which I was familiar and therefore comfortable. As I explored the idea, the realization of the links between the Sacred Heart and the heart in prayer became clear. The heart is the centre of the spiritual being and the place of prayer and, as such, is intimately linked with the heart of God—heart speaks to heart. The prayer of the heart is a concept especially connected to the Jesus Prayer in Orthodox Christianity, with the familiar idea of descending with the mind into the heart. St Theophan the Recluse teaches this in a well-known quotation from *The Way of the Pilgrim*:

> one must descend with the mind into the heart, and there stand before the face of the Lord, ever present, all seeing within you. The prayer takes a firm and steadfast hold, when a small fire begins to burn in the heart. Try not to quench this fire, and it will become established in such a way that the prayer repeats itself: and then you will have within you a small murmuring stream.[12]

---

[12] From *Откровенные рассказы странника духовному своему отцу* (Kazan, 1884), trans. Anna Zaranko, *The Way of the Pilgrim: Candid Tales of a Wanderer to His Spiritual Father*, introd. Andrew Louth (Penguin, 2017). Quoted in Henri Nouwen, *The Way of the Heart: Desert Spirituality and Contemporary Ministry* (Seabury Press, 1981), 76.

Although the term 'prayer of the heart' is associated very much with the Jesus Prayer, it is not limited to it. Prayer of the heart can be synonymous with contemplative prayer or silent prayer. The basic meaning is that it is prayer that happens when our heart touches the heart of God. It happens during the Eucharist when we enter fully and with presence into the Eucharistic action; it happens in the Divine Office when we give our whole attention and our presence to the Office. It happens in our silent times in Cell, Chapel or garden It can happen when we are not even aware of praying, in a heart that is totally devoted and given to God.

In Scripture the heart is the deepest element, the centre of the being, and the place of an individual's deepest feelings, emotions, and truth; whether that is of the human person or of God himself. To know a person's heart is to know them deeply, to win the heart of a person is to build a strong relationship of love with them.

We use the word 'heart' in many situations to describe deep connection: we have 'heart to heart' conversations; we 'pour out our heart' to someone; we suffer a broken heart. Medically there is such a thing as 'broken heart syndrome' occurring after severe emotional or physical stress.[13] When our heart ceases beating, we die; our spiritual heart, our innermost being, is just as vital. The definition given in the glossary to volume 1 of the *Philokalia* says that the heart …

> is not simply the physical organ but the spiritual centre of the human being, the person as made in the image of God, the deepest and truest self, the inner shrine, to be entered only through sacrifice and death, in which the mystery of the union of the divine and the human is consummated.[14]

---

[13] 'Takotsubo cardiomyopathy occurs when … the left ventricle, suddenly expands and weakens. This means that the heart can't pump blood around the body properly and this extra stress can lead to heart failure.' British Heart Foundation website, linked from this page: www.bhf.org.uk/ informationsupport/conditions/cardiomyopathy/, accessed 23 November 2023.

[14] Gerald E. H. Palmer, Philip Sherrard, and Kallistos Ware, ed. and trans., *The Philokalia: The Complete Text, compiled by St Nikodimos of the Holy Mountain and St Makarios of Corinth*, vol. 1 (Faber & Faber, 1979), 361–2.

Or as Henri Nouwen puts it: 'Prayer of the heart happens when the truth of who we are encounters the truth of who God is.'[15]

What does it mean to descend with the mind into the heart as the Orthodox church teaches? Some of the Orthodox Fathers took the idea very literally. The heart is the physical and spiritual organ of prayer, and they taught that we are literally to 'force' the prayer down from head to heart. There were a number of physical methods intended to help achieve this, including bodily postures and control of the breathing, most of which would probably seem extreme, unhelpful and even impossible for us now. However, awareness of breathing and even of the heartbeat can be helpful in prayer. A prayer word said silently in rhythm with the breath is a technique many use to still the mind, or even simply being aware of the action of breathing. We talk about the breath of life, and we often see the Holy Spirit as breath, as in the hymn 'Breathe on Me, Breath of God'.[16]

Also important in Orthodox teaching was the idea of warming the heart. Where the Holy Spirit is, there is fire, and a sense of physical warming in the region of the chest was a sign of the heart being warmed as the Prayer descended into it.

> They said to each other, 'Were not our hearts burning within us while he was talking to us on the road, while he was opening the scriptures to us?' (Luke 24:32).

This might put us in mind of teaching around the heart chakra: a balanced heart chakra in yoga is associated with love and with a balance in spiritual and physical desires. Our lives of devotion to the Incarnate Lord warm our hearts.

The Jesus Prayer is not a practice where one meditates on a particular mystery or even on the name of Jesus. However, it is vital that it is practised with a mindful awareness of the presence of God. It is kept from being vain repetition by the remembrance that we are in the presence of the Divine. The name of Jesus is not just a useful identifying label but brings the actual presence of the one named.

---

[15] Nouwen, *The Way of the Heart*, 31.

[16] Words by Edwin Hatch (1835–1889), *Hymns Ancient and Modern*, no. 157.

In Scripture, to know a person's name is to know that person intimately, as we see in the encounter between Manoah and his wife in Judges 13:18:

> And the Angel of the LORD said to him, 'Why do you ask My name, seeing it is wonderful?'

The King James Version translates this verse as:

> And the angel of the LORD said unto him, Why askest thou thus after my name, seeing it is secret?

A second way into the prayer of the heart is found in the teaching of the great Carmelites, St Teresa of Avila and St John of the Cross. Both recognized that the human being is multidimensional. We are aware of the idea of conscious and subconscious mind, but there is also the level of the heart where God dwells and touches us. Prayer is not about lovely experiences of undistracted peace, but about a connection with God deep in the being. Sometimes, just when we think that really nothing is going on in our prayer life, God may be at work in our innermost being, which can make us very bad judges of our own prayer life. A dry and distracted period of prayer may be the sign of God at work in our depths, while a period of delightful recollection could be the product of our own imagination. We simply do not have the ability to judge.

Teresa's description of the 'Interior Castle', with the soul making its way from the outer edges of the consciousness to the innermost, deepest depths where God dwells, is one illustration of this concept. She recognized that at times in prayer our inmost being may be deeply recollected, while our outer being, our thoughts and imagination, may be chaotic. She recognizes this with relief, explaining how her mind could be distracted but her spirit was nevertheless deeply in God. As she says in *The Interior Castle*:

> … there is an interior world here within us. Just as we cannot stop the movement of the heavens, but they proceed in rapid motion, so neither can we stop our mind; and then the faculties of the soul go with it, and we think that we are lost and have wasted the time spent before God. But the soul is perhaps completely joined with him in the dwelling places very close to the center while the mind

> is on the outskirts of the castle suffering from a thousand wild and poisonous beasts, and meriting by this suffering.[17]

For both Teresa and John, the discovery that God is present in the heart was revolutionary. John describes the delight of this realization in his commentary on Stanza 1 of the *Spiritual Canticle*; he goes on to say that it is the teaching that makes sense of everything:

> We must remember that the Word, the Son of God, together with the Father and the Holy Spirit, is hidden in essence and in presence, in the inmost being of the soul. That soul, therefore, that will find Him, must go out from all things in will and affection, and enter into the profoundest self-recollection, and all things must be to it as if they existed not. … Courage, then, O soul most beautiful, you know now that your Beloved, Whom you desire, dwells hidden within your breast; strive, therefore, to be truly hidden with Him, and then you shall embrace Him, and be conscious of His presence with loving affection.[18]

Teresa uses the term 'mental prayer'. The terminology can be an issue for us with our modern concept that mental is 'of the mind'. She is in fact teaching a way to the heart: prayer that is not simply on the lips but in the heart. She was writing and teaching at a difficult time in church history, when the church leadership saw contemplative prayer as something for the spiritual elite, not for the layperson and certainly not for women, who should just be satisfied with their vocal prayers. Teresa did agree with them over the importance of vocal prayers, but only when they are said properly: in *The Way of Perfection* she states that we should 'say our prayers well' and in so doing we enter into mental or contemplative prayer:

> Realise daughters that the nature of mental prayer isn't determined by whether or not the mouth is closed. If while speaking I thoroughly understand and know that I am speaking of God

[17] *The Interior Castle*, IV, chapter 1, para. 9, trans. Kavanaugh, Op. cit. 320.

[18] Saint John of the Cross, *A Spiritual Canticle of the Soul and the Bridegroom Christ*, stanza 1, para. 12, trans. David Lewis and Benedict Zimmerman OCD, modernized by Harry Plantinga (Christian Classics Ethereal Library, 1995), 20–1.

> and I have a greater awareness of this than I do of the words I'm saying, mental and vocal prayer are joined. If however, others tell you that they are speaking with God while reciting the Our Father and at the same time thinking of the world, then I have nothing to say.[19]

Thus, in fact, those vocal prayers with which the leadership felt women should be solely concerned are a direct way into the prayer of the heart, so Teresa subverts the authorities. She is advocating a move from the head to the heart, the traditional place of encounter with God.

The Jesus Prayer has a similar progression, first learning the words and the discipline of repeating them at set times and places and then more freely during the day.[20] As we practise the Jesus Prayer we encounter our scattered, distracted minds and our tendency to forget the prayer and drift away. However, gradually the Prayer becomes more habitual, easier and quicker to return to when we drift, more often there in the corners of our mind, perhaps even greeting us when we wake. Eventually the prayer descends into our hearts.

Prayer of the mind in the heart is prayer in the depth of our being and, as the Desert Fathers recognized, is a journey we can make during our spiritual life. As we deepen in our practice of prayer, we move from saying prayers to being prayer. Saying prayer remains important—Office, the words of the Mass, vocal prayers—but the depth of our engagement with God moves from exterior practice to interior presence. At the same time, the saying of the words themselves can begin to take us straight to the heart. I remember Father Gregory CSWG commenting on Sister Hilda Mary when she was elderly and rather confused: 'She can no longer decide to pray, she is prayer.'

---

[19] *The Way of Perfection*, chapter 22, para. 1, trans. Kieran Kavanaugh OCD, Otilio Rodriguez OCD, *The Collected Works of St. Teresa of Avila*, vol. 2 (Institute of Carmelite Studies, 1976), 121.

[20] One of our recent publications offers an introduction to praying with the Jesus Prayer for those who have not used it before: Bruce Batstone, *Still Listening: Sowing the Seeds of the Jesus Prayer*, Fairacres Publications 206 (SLG Press, 2023).

I would like to close by reiterating the quotation from Father Cary's *Anima Christi* retreat, to emphasize the idea of bringing the sacred humanity of Jesus into the forefront of our lives. The prayer of the heart takes us straight into this intimate relationship with God, through which we see the world as God sees it, and as a result turn our lives to love, intercession, and holiness.

> We find our way of access to the Heart of Jesus most truly in our intensive life of prayer. That is what is procured for us in so far as we have entered in any way whatever upon a life of contemplation, through bringing the Sacred Humanity of Jesus into the forefront of our life ... it is in the Heart of Jesus, Jesus as He is in His Glory, that we find set before us the vision of the Life and Love of God ... there is no short-cut to this intimacy with the sacred Heart. ... It is here in this kind of intimacy with the Heart of Jesus, this most holy state where the Precious Blood does its most perfect work within the ransomed life, that there is found that Christ-like perception of the needs and sorrows of the world which He has ransomed, and of the character and power of the Love of God to Whom we are redeemed.

Sister Clare-Louise SLG worked as a nurse and then qualified as a librarian in the University of Wales before entering the Sisters of the Love of God. She was one of the authors of *Monastic Vocation* (SLG Press, 2021) and is a frequent contributor to the *Fairacres Chronicle* in addition to her preface to each issue as current Reverend Mother of the Sisters of the Love of God. She is influenced and encouraged by the Carmelite Saints and gives talks and retreats on the subject.

SLG PRESS PUBLICATIONS

FP1	*Prayer and the Life of Reconciliation*	Gilbert Shaw (1969)
FP2	*Aloneness Not Loneliness*	Mother Mary Clare SLG (1969)
FP4	*Intercession*	Mother Mary Clare SLG (1969)
FP8	*Prayer: Extracts from the Teaching of Fr Gilbert Shaw*	Gilbert Shaw (1973)
FP12	*Learning to Pray*	Mother Mary Clare SLG (1970)
FP15	*Death, the Gateway to Life*	Gilbert Shaw (1971, 3/2024)
FP16	*The Victory of the Cross*	Dumitru Stăniloae (1970, 3/2023)
FP26	*The Message of Saint Seraphim*	Irina Gorainov (1974)
FP28	*Julian of Norwich: Four Studies to Commemorate the Sixth Centenary of the Revelations of Divine Love*	Sister Benedicta Ward SLG, Sister Eileen Mary SLG, Sister Mary Paul SLG, A. M. Allchin (1973, 3/2022)
FP43	*The Power of the Name: The Jesus Prayer in Orthodox Spirituality*	Kallistos Ware (1974)
FP46	*Prayer and Contemplation* and *Distractions are for Healing*	Robert Llewelyn (1975, 2/2024)
FP48	*The Wisdom of the Desert Fathers*	trans. Sister Benedicta Ward SLG (1975)
FP50	*Letters of Saint Antony the Great*	trans. Derwas Chitty (1975, 2/2021)
FP54	*From Loneliness to Solitude*	Roland Walls (1976)
FP55	*Theology and Spirituality*	Andrew Louth (1976, rev. 1978, 3/2024)
FP61	*Kabir: The Way of Love and Paradox*	Sister Rosemary SLG (1977)
FP62	*Anselm of Canterbury: A Monastic Scholar*	Sister Benedicta Ward SLG (1973, 2/2024)
FP67	*Mary and the Mystery of the Incarnation: An Essay on the Mother of God in the Theology of Karl Barth*	Andrew Louth (1977, 2/2024)
FP68	*Trinity and Incarnation in Anglican Tradition*	A. M. Allchin (1977, 2/2024)
FP70	*Facing Depression*	Gonville ffrench-Beytagh (1978, 2/2020)
FP71	*The Single Person*	Philip Welsh (1979)
FP72	*The Letters of Ammonas, Successor of St Antony*	trans. Derwas Chitty, introd. Sebastian Brock (1979, 2/2023)
FP74	*George Herbert, Priest and Poet*	Kenneth Mason (1980)
FP75	*A Study of Wisdom: Three Tracts by the Author of* The Cloud of Unknowing	trans. Clifton Wolters (1980)
FP81	*The Psalms: Prayer Book of the Bible*	Dietrich Bonhoeffer, trans. Sister Isabel SLG (1982)
FP82	*Prayer & Holiness: The Icon of Man Renewed in God*	Dumitru Stăniloae (1982, rev. 2023)
FP85	*Walter Hilton: Eight Chapters on Perfection & Angels' Song*	trans. Rosemary Dorward (1983, rev. 3/2024)
FP88	*Creative Suffering*	Iulia de Beausobre (1989)
FP90	*Bringing Forth Christ: Five Feasts of the Child Jesus by St Bonaventure*	trans. Eric Doyle OFM (1984, 3/2024)
FP92	*Gentleness in John of the Cross*	Thomas Kane (1985)
FP94	*Saint Gregory Nazianzen: Selected Poems*	trans. John McGuckin (1986, 2/2024)
FP95	*The World of the Desert Fathers: Stories & Sayings from the Anonymous Series of the* Apophthegmata Patrum	trans. Columba Stewart OSB (1986, 2/2020)
FP104	*Growing Old with God*	Timothy N. Rudd (1988, 2/2020)

FP105 *The Simplicity of Prayer: Extracts from the Teaching of Mother Mary Clare* SLG
Mother Mary Clare SLG (1988, 2/2024)
FP106 *Julian Reconsidered* Kenneth Leech, Sister Benedicta Ward SLG (1988/ rev. 2/2024)
FP108 *The Unicorn: Meditations on the Love of God* Harry Galbraith Miller (1989)
FP109 *The Creativity of Diminishment* Sister Anke (1990)
FP110 *Called to be Priests* Hugh Wybrew (1989, 2/2024)
FP111 *A Kind of Watershed: An Anglican Lay View of Sacramental Confession*
Christine North (1990, 2/2022)
FP116 *Jesus, the Living Lord* Bp Michael Ramsey (1992)
FP120 *The Monastic Letters of Saint Athanasius the Great*
trans. and introd. Leslie Barnard (1994, 2/2023)
FP122 *The Hidden Joy* Sister Jane SLG, ed. Dorothy Sutherland (1994)
FP124 *Prayer of the Heart: An Approach to Silent Prayer and Prayer in the Night*
Alexander Ryrie (1995, 3/2020)
FP125 *Whole Christ: The Spirituality of Ministry* Philip Seddon (1996)
FP126 *Evelyn Underhill, Anglican Mystic: Two Centenary Essays*
A. M. Allchin, Bp Michael Ramsey (1977, 3/2024)
FP127 *Apostolate and the Mirrors of Paradox*
Sydney Evans, ed. Andrew Linzey & Brian Horne (1996)
FP128 *The Wisdom of Saint Isaac the Syrian* Sebastian Brock (1997)
FP129 *Saint Thérèse of Lisieux: Her Relevance for Today* Sister Eileen Mary SLG (1997)
FP130 *Expectations: Five Addresses for Those Beginning Ministry* Sister Edmée SLG (1997, 2/2024)
FP131 *Scenes from Animal Life: Fables for the Enneagram Types*
Waltraud Kirschke, trans. Sister Isabel SLG (1998)
FP132 *Praying the Word of God: The Use of* Lectio Divina Charles Dumont OCSO (1999)
FP133 *Love Unknown: Meditations on the Death and Resurrection of Jesus*
John Barton (1999, 2/2024)
FP134 *The Hidden Way of Love: Jean-Pierre de Caussade's Spirituality of Abandonment*
Barry Conaway (1999, 2/2024)
FP135 *Shepherd and Servant: The Spiritual Theology of Saint Dunstan* Douglas Dales (2000)
FP137 *Pilgrimage of the Heart* Sister Benedicta Ward SLG (2001)
FP138 *Mixed Life* Walter Hilton, trans. Rosemary Dorward (2001, 2/2024)
FP139 *In the Footsteps of the Lord: The Teaching of Abba Isaiah of Scetis*
John Chryssavgis, Luke Penkett (2001, 2/2023)
FP140 *A Great Joy: Reflections on the Meaning of Christmas* Kenneth Mason (2001)
FP141 *Bede and the Psalter* Sister Benedicta Ward SLG (2002, 2/2024)
FP142 *Abhishiktananda: A Memoir of Dom Henri Le Saux* Murray Rogers, David Barton (2003)
FP143 *Friendship in God: The Encounter of Evelyn Underhill & Sorella Maria of Campello*
A. M. Allchin (2003, 2/2024)
FP144 *Christian Imagination in Poetry and Polity: Some Anglican Voices from Temple to Herbert*
Bp Rowan Williams (2004)
FP145 *The Reflections of Abba Zosimas: Monk of the Palestinian Desert*
trans. and introd. John Chryssavgis (2005, 3/2022)
FP146 *The Gift of Theology: The Trinitarian Vision of Ann Griffiths and Elizabeth of Dijon*
A. M. Allchin (2005)
FP147 *Sacrifice and Spirit* Bp Michael Ramsey (2005)
FP148 *Saint John Cassian on Prayer* trans. A. M Casiday (2006, 2/2024)
FP149 *Hymns of Saint Ephrem the Syrian* trans. Mary Hansbury (2006, 2/2024)

FP150 *Suffering: Why All this Suffering? What Do I Do about It?*
Reinhard Körner OCD, trans. Sister Avis Mary SLG (2006)
FP151 *A True Easter: The Synod of Whitby 664 AD* Sister Benedicta Ward SLG (2007)
FP152 *Prayer as Self-Offering* Alexander Ryrie (2007)
FP153 *From Perfection to the Elixir: How George Herbert Fashioned a Famous Poem*
Benedick de la Mare (2008, 2/2024)
FP154 *The Jesus Prayer: Gospel Soundings* Sister Pauline Margaret CHN (2008)
FP155 *Loving God Whatever: Through the Year with Sister Jane* Sister Jane SLG (2006)
FP156 *Prayer and Meditation for a Sleepless Night*
Sisters of the Love of God (1993, 3/2024)
FP157 *Being There: Caring for the Bereaved* John Porter (2009)
FP158 *Learn to Be at Peace: The Practice of Stillness* Andrew Norman (2010)
FP159 *From Holy Week to Easter* George Pattison (2010)
FP160 *Strength in Weakness: The Scandal of the Cross* John W. Rogerson (2010)
FP161 *Augustine Baker: Frontiers of the Spirit* Victor de Waal (2010, 2/2024)
FP162 *Out of the Depths*
Gonville ffrench-Beytagh; epilogue Wendy Robinson (1990, 2/2010)
FP163 *God and Darkness: A Carmelite Perspective*
Gemma Hinricher OCD, trans. Sister Avis Mary SLG (2010)
FP164 *The Gift of Joy* Curtis Almquist SSJE (2011)
FP165 *'I Have Called You Friends': Suggestions for the Spiritual Life Based on the Farewell Discourses of Jesus* Reinhard Körner OCD (2012)
FP166 *Leisure* Mother Mary Clare SLG (2012)
FP167 *Carmelite Ascent: An Introduction to Saint Teresa and Saint John of the Cross*
Mother Mary Clare SLG (1973, rev. 2012)
FP168 *Ann Griffiths and Her Writings* Llewellyn Cumings (2012)
FP169 *The Our Father* Sister Benedicta Ward SLG (2012)
FP171 *The Spiritual Wisdom of the Syriac Book of Steps* Robert A. Kitchen (2013)
FP172 *The Prayer of Silence* Alexander Ryrie (2012)
FP173 *On Tour in Byzantium: Excerpts from The Spiritual Meadow of John Moschus*
Ralph Martin SSM (2013)
FP174 *Monastic Life* Bonnie Thurston (2016)
FP175 *Shall All Be Well? Reflections for Holy Week* Graham Ward (2015)
FP176 *Solitude and Communion: Papers on the Hermit Life* ed. A. M. Allchin (2015)
FP177 *The Prayers of Jacob of Serugh* ed. Mary Hansbury (2015)
FP178 *The Monastic Hours of Prayer* Sister Benedicta Ward SLG (2016)
FP179 *The Desert of the Heart: Daily Readings with the Desert Fathers*
trans. Sister Benedicta Ward SLG (2016)
FP180 *In Company with Christ: Lent, Palm Sunday, Good Friday & Easter to Pentecost*
Sister Benedicta Ward SLG (2016)
FP181 *Lazarus: Come Out! Reflections on John 11* Bonnie Thurston (2017)
FP182 *Unknowing & Astonishment: Meditations on Faith for the Long Haul*
Christopher Scott (2018)
FP183 *Pondering, Praying, Preaching: Romans 8* Bonnie Thurston (2019, 2/2021)
FP184 *Shem`on the Graceful: Discourse on the Solitary Life*
trans. and introd. Mary Hansbury (2020)
FP185 *God Under My Roof: Celtic Songs and Blessings* Esther de Waal (2020)
FP186 *Journeying with the Jesus Prayer* James F. Wellington (2020)

FP187 *Poet of the Word: Re-reading Scripture with Ephraem the Syrian* Aelred Partridge OC (2020)
FP188 *Identity and Ritual* Alan Griffiths (2021)
FP189 *River of the Spirit: The Spirituality of Simon Barrington-Ward* Andy Lord (2021)
FP190 *Prayer and the Struggle against Evil* John Barton, Daniel Lloyd, James Ramsay, Alexander Ryrie (2021)
FP191 *Dante's Spiritual Journey: A Reading of the Divine Comedy* Tony Dickinson (2021)
FP192 *Jesus the Undistorted Image of God* John Townroe (2022)
FP193 *Our Deepest Desire: Prayer, Fasting & Almsgiving in the Writings of Saint Augustine of Hippo* Sister Susan SLG (2022)
FP194 *Lent with George Herbert* Tony Dickinson (2022)
FP195 *Four Ways to the Cross* Tony Dickinson (2022)
FP196 *Anselm of Canterbury, Teacher of Prayer* Sister Benedicta Ward SLG (2022)
FP197 *With One Heart and Mind: Prayers out of Stillness* Anthony Kemp (2023)
FP198 *Sayings of the Urban Fathers & Mothers* James Ashdown (2023)
FP199 *Doors* Sister Raphael SLG (2023)
FP200 *Monastic Vocation* Sisters of the Love of God, Bp Rowan Williams (2021)
FP201 *An Ecology of the Heart: Faith Through the Climate Crisis* Duncan Forbes (2023)
FP202 *'In the image of the Image': Gregory of Nyssa's Opposition to Slavery* Adam Couchman (2023)
FP203 *Gregory of Nyssa and the Sins of Asia Minor* Jonathan Farrugia (2023)
FP204 *Discovery* Arthur Bell (2023)
FP205 *Living Healing: the Spirituality of Leanne Payne* Andy Lord (2023)
FP206 *Still Listening: Sowing the Seeds of the Jesus Prayer* Bruce Batstone CJN (2023)
FP207 *Julian of Norwich: Four Essays to Commemorate 650 Years of the* Revelations of Divine Love Bp Graham Usher, Father Colin CSWG, Sister Elizabeth Ruth Obbard OC, Mother Hilary Crupi OJN (2023)
FP208 *Time* Dumitru Stăniloae, Kallistos Ware (2023)
FP209 *Pearls of Life: A Lifebelt for the Spirit* Tony Dickinson (2024)
FP210 *The Way and the Truth and the Life: An Exploration by a Follower of the Way* James Ramsay (2024)
FP211 *Cosmos, Crisis & Christ: Essays of Wendy Robinson* Wendy Robinson (2024)
FP212 *Towards a Theology of Psychotherapy: The Spirituality of Wendy Robinson* Andrew Louth (2024)
FP213 *Immersed in God and the World: Living Priestly Ministry* Andy Lord (2024)
FP214 *The Road to Emmaus: A Sculptor's Journey through Time* Rodney Munday (2024)
FP215 *Prayer Too Deep for Words* Sister Edmée SLG (2024)
FP216 *The Prayers of St Isaac of Nineveh* Sebastian Brock (2024)
FP217 *Two Medieval English Saints: Cuthbert and Alban* Sister Benedicta Ward SLG (2024)
FP218 *Encountering the Depths* Mother Mary Clare SLG (1981, rev. 3/2024)
FP219 *Conflict and Concord* Sister Susan SLG, Bp Humphrey Southern, Bronwen Neil, Sister Rosemary SLG, Sister Clare-Louise SLG (2024)
FP220 *Zeal for the Faith: An Introduction to Christian-Muslim Dialogue* Tony Dickinson (2024)
FP221 *Divine Love in the Song of Songs* Sister Edmée SLG (2024)

Contemplative Poetry series

CP1	*Amado Nervo: Poems of Faith and Doubt*	trans. John Gallas (2021)
CP2	*Anglo-Saxon Poets: The High Roof of Heaven*	trans. John Gallas (2021)
CP3	*Middle English Poets: Where Grace Grows Ever Green*	ed. John Gallas (2021)
CP4	*Selected Poems: The Voice inside Our Home*	Edward Clarke (2022)
CP5	*Women & God: Drops in the Sea of Time*	trans. and ed. John Gallas (2022)
CP6	*Gabrielle de Coignard & Vittoria Colonna: Fly Not Too High*	trans. John Gallas (2022)
CP7	*Selected Poems: Chancing on Sanctity*	James Ramsay (2022)
CP8	*Gabriela Mistral: This Far Place*	trans. John Gallas (2023)
CP9	*Henry Vaughan & George Herbert: Divine Themes and Celestial Praise*	ed. Edward Clarke (2023)
CP10	*Love Will Come with Fire*	Sisters of the Love of God (2023)
CP11	*Touchpapers*	coll. and trans. John Gallas (2023)
CP12	*Seasons of my Soul*	Clare McKerron (2023)
CP13	*Reinhard Sorge: Take Flight to God*	trans. John Gallas (2024)
CP14	*Embertide: Encountering Saint Frideswide*	Romola Parish (2024)
CP15	*Thomas Campion: Made All of Light*	ed. Julia Craig-McFeely (2024)

Vestry Guides

VG1	*The Visiting Minister: How to Welcome Visiting Clergy to Your Church*	Paul Monk (2021)
VG2	*Help! No Minister! or Please Take the Service*	Paul Monk (2022)
VG3	*The Liturgy of the Eucharist: An Introductory Guide*	Paul Monk (2024)

www.slgpress.co.uk